D1502224

Books for Children of the World

Books for Children of the World
The Story of Jella Lepman

For Marianne —
I hope you enjoy this story.
— Sydelle Pearl

By Sydelle Pearl
Illustrated by Danlyn Iantorno

PELICAN PUBLISHING COMPANY
Gretna 2007

For my mother, Ruth Pearl

*Many thanks to Anne Marie Mortara for sharing photographs of her mother,
Jella (pronounced "Yella") Lepman. Thanks also to Leena Maissen and Meena
Khorana for initial research suggestions. —S. P.*

*To Roberta Collier-Morales, the art teacher who made a difference, and to
Lou, Chandler, and Taylor for helping me live my dream. —D. I.*

Text copyright © 2007
By Sydelle Pearl

Illustrations copyright © 2007
By Danlyn Iantorno
All rights reserved

*The word "Pelican" and the depiction of a pelican are
trademarks of Pelican Publishing Company, Inc., and
are registered in the U.S. Patent and Trademark Office.*

Library of Congress Cataloging-in-Publication Data

Pearl, Sydelle.
  Books for children of the world : the story of Jella Lepman / by Sydelle Pearl ; illustrated by
Danlyn Iantorno.
       p. cm.
  Includes bibliographical references.
  ISBN-13: 978-1-58980-438-8 (alk. paper)
  1. Lepman, Jella—Juvenile literature. 2. Children's librarians—Germany—Biography—
Juvenile literature. 3. Children—Books and reading—Juvenile literature. 4. Children's liter-
ature—Exhibitions—Juvenile literature. 5. Internationale Jugendbibliothek (Munich,
Germany)—History—Juvenile literature. 6. Children's libraries—Germany—Munich—
History—20th century—Juvenile literature. 7. Reconstruction (1939-1951)—Germany—
Juvenile literature. I. Iantorno, Danlyn, ill. II. Title.
  Z720.L46P43 2007
  028.5'5—dc22
                                                  2006031109

"The cover illustration from **THE STORY OF FERDINAND** *by Munro Leaf, illustrated by
Robert Lawson, copyright 1936 by Munro Leaf and Robert Lawson, renewed (c) 1964 by Munro
Leaf and John W. Boyd, is used by permission of Viking Penguin, A Division of Penguin Young
Reader's Group, A Member of Penguin Group (USA) Inc., 345 Hudson Street, New York, NY
10014. All rights reserved."*

Printed in China
Published by Pelican Publishing Company, Inc.
1000 Burmaster Street, Gretna, Louisiana 70053

BOOKS FOR CHILDREN OF THE WORLD: THE STORY OF JELLA LEPMAN

One December night in 1946 a woman named Jella Lepman sat on the steps of the International Exhibition of Children's Books in Berlin. The wind blew her hair all around and rustled the pages of the book on her lap, but Jella did not seem to notice. She was thinking about the children who waited in long lines to climb up the steps into the big room to see the books.

Many of them wore thin coats and stuffed newspapers into their shoes to keep their feet warm because they had no boots. They walked carefully around holes in the street where bombs had fallen during the Second World War. But now the war was over.

Soon it would be Christmas, but the children would not receive gifts this year because their families had no money. When they came to the exhibition, they asked for the books as Christmas presents. Jella wished she could think of a way to give books to the children.

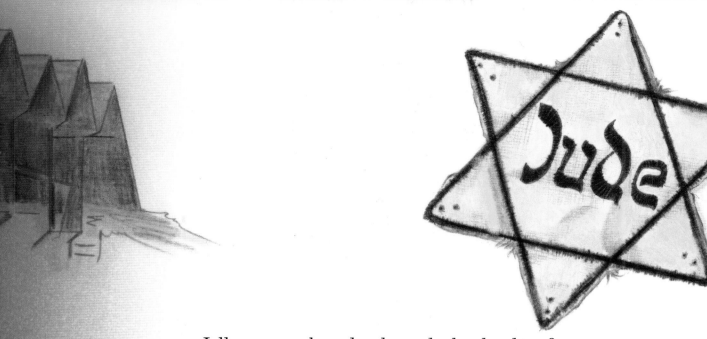

Jella remembered when dark clouds of war hung over Germany. From 1933 to 1945, the Nazi government declared that only books written in German could stay on the shelves of schools and libraries. Books in other languages and books showing people of different cultures were taken away and burned. Books about soldiers marching off to war and books telling terrible lies about Jews were added to the shelves.

Jewish people had to wear a yellow star on their clothes. They could not go to parks, libraries, or public schools. It was not safe for them to live in Germany. Those who stayed were taken from their homes the way that unwanted books were removed from the shelves. Jella, who was Jewish, escaped to London, England, with her son and daughter. There, she wrote news stories for England and the United States.

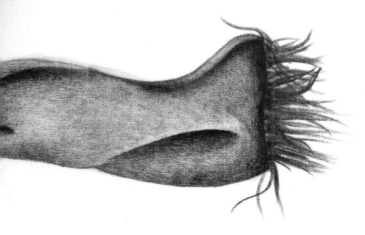

When the war was over in 1945, the government in Germany changed. Books showing marching soldiers and books telling lies about the Jewish people were taken out of schools and libraries. Books in different languages and about other cultures were welcomed. But there was not enough money, ink, or paper to print them.

After the war, the United States Army asked Jella to return to Germany to find out what children needed in order to live better lives. At first Jella was afraid to return. But she knew that she wanted German children to have a peaceful future, so she bravely boarded a plane that would take her back to Germany. On the airplane from London, Jella felt as though she were falling upside down and she closed her eyes.

In Germany, Jella rode in an army jeep that had bouncy seats. She pointed on a map to places she wanted to go, and Joe, her driver, took her there.

One place they went to was the city of Stuttgart, where Jella had lived before the war. Buildings had fallen down because bombs had been dropped on them, but Jella remembered when they stood up straight and tall.

As the weeks went by and the jeep clattered over the frozen streets of Germany, Jella thought about the children she met. They needed homes, clothes, shoes, and coal. They were hungry for food. But they were also hungry for books. Jella knew she had to find a way to get books for the children.

At army headquarters, Jella wore her major's uniform when she spoke to General McClure. Her heart pounded as she explained her idea of having an exhibition of children's books from around the world that would travel through Germany. She was told that there was no money, but Jella wanted to try to get the books without money. Then she was told that the countries that had been at war with Germany would not want to send books.

But Jella replied, "If the war really is over, if one is to believe in peaceful coexistence, the first messengers of that peace will be these children's books." General McClure agreed and Jella left the room feeling like her shoes had grown wings.

One night when the officers left army headquarters, Jella began to type letters to publishing
houses. A soldier asked her what she was doing.
Jella couldn't tell him that she was trying to get
books for children because it would not have
sounded important enough. She pretended that a
certain officer had given her a lot of typing to do
and the soldier left her alone.

Little by little, night after night, Jella typed
letters to publishing houses in twenty countries.
She asked for books with pictures because the
pictures would help tell the stories. Jella asked
that paintings by children be sent along too.
Finally, she finished typing the letters and
mailed them. Now she had to wait and see if she
would get any letters back.

The first letter—a "dove of peace" Jella called it—came from France. She ran to show General McClure before she opened it. It said that French publishers would send books!

Other countries wrote back. Books in different languages and paintings by children arrived. Jella remembered how she hung the paintings in the traveling exhibition so that children would see them as soon as they entered. One girl pointed to a picture of Santa with his reindeer sleigh and said softly, "Oh, now it is peace."

Happily the children opened the books but sadly closed them when told they could not take them home. Some pages were wrinkled and ripped where nearly a million hands had touched them. The books had traveled to Munich, Stuttgart, Frankfurt, and now Berlin. Many children hugged the books and even kissed the covers.

One book was in English and came from the United States. It was about a bull named Ferdinand who didn't want to fight. He loved to sit under a tree and smell the flowers. This was the book Jella held in her lap as she sat on the steps of the exhibition hall in Berlin.

Suddenly, she had a wonderful idea. She would translate *The Story of Ferdinand* from English into German! Then she would go to her friends at the Tempelhof printing press and ask them to print copies on newspapers of the German words with pictures from the American book. She could give away the newspaper books as Christmas presents to the children!

Jella picked up *Ferdinand,* rushed inside the exhibition hall and reached for a pencil and some paper. The snowflakes fell as she wrote, changing Ferdinand the Bull to Ferdinand der Stier. When she was finished, the snow twinkled like diamonds in the moonlight.

Jella went to see her friends at the Tempelhof printing press. Through the night, thirty thousand newspaper copies of *Ferdinand* were printed. Jella could hardly sleep!

A few days before Christmas, Jella gave a newsprint copy of *Ferdinand* to each delighted child at the exhibition. The grownups who came with the children thanked her again and again.

Jella wished to create a library with books from the exhibition. The library would be built in Germany and would be a gift for the children of the world. Two men from the Rockefeller Foundation in New York visited the exhibition in Berlin. They told her to apply for money through the foundation to help her build her library.

One day in 1948, Jella received a letter from the Rockefeller Foundation inviting her to come to the United States to speak about children's books and visit with librarians and publishers to gather support for her library.

Jella arrived at the airport in Munich with great excitement as she dared to realize her dream. A newspaper reporter asked her, "Will you be traveling alone?"

"Indeed not," she said, thinking of the children who wished for books. "Thousands of children starving for books are flying along with me."

In New York, Jella saw the marble lions in front of the New York Public Library. Children of many cultures sat inside reading books the way that she hoped children would one day sit in her library in Germany.

She wore a new hat with flowers the day she made a new friend, Mildred L. Batchelder, a librarian who believed that children's books from many lands should be translated into English for American children.

Another friend Jella made was Eleanor Roosevelt, wife of President Franklin D. Roosevelt. When Eleanor wrote a newspaper article about Jella's need for books and money for her library, many people sent book packages and checks. Jella also received grant money from the Rockefeller Foundation to build her library.

On September 14, 1949, children wearing their best clothes walked into the International Youth Library for the first time. Some children read aloud from their favorite books. *The Adventures of Pinocchio* was read in Italian, *Heidi* was read in Swiss, *The Story of Babar* was read in French, *Emil and the Detectives* was read in German, and *The Story of Ferdinand* was read in English.

All across Germany, people listened on their radios. Many children remembered the newspaper copies of *Ferdinand* that Jella had given them for Christmas almost three years before.

Books in different languages sat side by side on the shelves of the library the way that children from different cultures sat side by side in the chairs. Jella believed that each book in another language helped to build a bridge of peace.

AUTHOR'S NOTE

After the Nazi government under Adolf Hitler was defeated in 1945, Germany and the city of Berlin were divided into zones and occupied by the Americans, French, British, and Soviets. Jella became "advisor on the cultural and educational needs of women and children in the American zone," as she relates in her book, *A Bridge of Children's Books*. As the advisor, she coordinated the International Exhibition of Children's Books, which opened in Munich in July 1946, traveled to Stuttgart in August, Frankfurt in October, and then Berlin in December. By the time the exhibition closed, about a million people had seen the books.

In her lecture tour to the United States, Jella visited New York City, St. Louis, and Chicago, home of the American Library Association. Librarian Mildred L. Batchelder helped enormously with the administration of the Rockefeller Foundation grant and remained invested in the future of the International Youth Library (IYL).

Since 1953, the IYL has been supported by the United Nations agency UNESCO. It is also funded by the Bavarian State Ministry for Education and Culture and the Bavarian capital city of Munich. It has been located in Munich's Blutenberg Castle since 1983. A picture of the IYL appears at the beginning of this book. The research collection contains 500,000 children's books in more than 130 languages, and the lending collection is comprised of 20,000 children's books in 13 languages. Books are still donated by various countries.

In 1953, Jella founded the International Board on Books for Young People (IBBY), an organization for children's book specialists worldwide. IBBY sponsors conferences and publishes a journal called *Bookbird*.

Jella Lepman died in Zurich, Switzerland, on October 5, 1970, at the age of seventy-nine. All quotes from my book come from Jella's book, *A Bridge of Children's Books*.

SELECTED SOURCES

Betten, Liobba, ed. *Mrs. Lepman: Give Us Books, Give Us Wings.* Munich: Romen Kovar Verlag, 1992.

Hazard, Paul. *Books, Children and Men.* Trans. Marguerite Mitchell. Boston: Horn Book, Inc., 1944.

Kamenetsky, Christa. *Children's Literature in Hitler's Germany: The Cultural Policy of National Socialism.* Ohio and London: Ohio University Press, 1984.

Leaf, Munro. *The Story of Ferdinand.* Ill. Robert Lawson. New York: Viking Press, 1936.

Lepman, Jella. *A Bridge of Children's Books.* ALA (American Library Association), Chicago and Leicester, England: Brockhampton Press, 1969. Republished in 2002 by the O'Brien Press in association with IBBY Ireland and USBBY.

For more information about the organization IBBY, visit www.ibby.org.
Visit www.ijb.de for more information about the Internationale
Jugendbibliothek, the International Youth Library.